D0585091

First published in the UK in 2004 by
Chrysalis Children's Books
An imprint of Chrysalis Books Group Plc
The Chrysalis Building, Bramley Road,
London W10 6SP

ISBN 1 84458 114 4

British Library Cataloguing in Publication Data for this
book is available from the British Library.

Editorial Manager *Joyce Bentley*
Editorial Assistant *Camilla Lloyd*
Produced by Tall Tree Ltd
Designer *Ed Simkins*
Editor *Kate Simkins*
Consultant *Jon Kirkwood*
Picture Researcher *Lorna Ainger*

Printed in China

Some of the more unfamiliar words used in this book
are explained in the glossary on page 31.

Typography *Natascha Frensch*
Read Regular, READ SMALLCAPS and Read Space;
European Community Design Registration 2003 and
Copyright © Natascha Frensch 2001-2004
Read Medium, Read Black and *Read Slanted*
Copyright © Natascha Frensch 2003-2004

READ™ is a revolutionary new typeface that will enchance
children's understanding through clear, easily recognisable
character shapes. With its evenly spaced and carefully
designed characters, READ™ will help children at all stages
to improve their literacy skills, and is ideal for young readers,
reluctant readers and especially children with dyslexia.

Photo Credits
The publishers would like to thank the following for their kind permission
to reproduce the photographs:

Alamy.com: Adrian Chinery 17t, Vick Fisher 5t, Robert Harding World Imagery
4, 8, 28bl, Napper/The Flight Collection 25t, Dave Pattison 15b, Popperfoto
7t, 23b, David Sanger 15t The Art Archive: National Anthropological Museum
Mexico / Dagli Orti 6 Courtesy British Aerospace 23t, front cover tr Corbis:
Bettmann 12, 18, 20, 28tr, Richard Cummins 16, Milepost 92 9t, Stapleton
Collection 5b, 7b, Joel Stettenheim 9b Courtesy Cunard: 17b, 28-9, back cover
Courtesy dg-flugzeugbau.de: 1, 21b, 30 Digital Vision: 11, 31, front cover c, br
Getty Images: AFP 19t, Kean Collection 25b, Greg Mathieson/Mai 19b, Susan
Muhlhauser 14, National Archives 22, 29bl, Kazuhiro Nogi 24, Hrvoje Polan
13t, Rischgitz 10, front cover tl, Time Life Pictures 27, Alex Wong 21t
Courtesy Mercedes: 13b, front cover bl NASA: 2, 26l, 26-7, 29tr, bl

Contents

Animal helpers

Humans have always walked from place to place. Over the years, people started to use animals as transport, such as dogs, elephants and camels.

Animals have been used to carry loads and people for thousands of years. The earliest such animals were horses and dogs. Wild dogs were first tamed and used as pack animals by humans nearly 12 000 years ago.

◀ Sledges are the oldest known vehicles. They are still used in icy regions of the world.

LOOK CLOSER

The camel is an ideal pack animal for the desert. To stop sand from getting in its face, it has long eyelashes, hairy ears and a nose that can close. It also has a hump on its back that acts as a store for its food and water.

The first people carried nothing with them as they moved around. As humans started to have more possessions, such as tools, they also needed something to carry them around in. As a result, they developed simple vehicles, such as sledges, that could be dragged by hand or by animals.

▼ A litter is a bed or couch that is carried by people or animals.

On wheels

The invention of the wheel was a major advance that revolutionised transport. It led to the development of many vehicles and machines that allowed people to travel more easily.

The wheel has proved to be one of the most useful inventions. Not only are vehicles equipped with wheels to help them move more easily, but wheels also form the basis of machines such as water wheels, clocks and factory machinery.

▼ Before the wheel was invented, rollers made out of logs were used. These made the movement of heavy loads easier.

The first wheels were solid wooden discs. Over the years, the wheel has been improved with the introduction of spokes and tyres. Early tyres were metal rings that protected the outside of the wheel. In the 19th century, air-filled rubber tyres were invented. These helped cushion the wheel, making rides more comfortable.

▶ The first rubber tyres, like those on this penny-farthing bicycle of the 19th century, were solid rubber.

EUREKA!

The earliest pictures of wheels date from Ancient Sumeria around 3500 BC. About 1500 years later, spoked wheels were invented. These were lighter and allowed vehicles, such the Ancient Egyptian chariot shown here, to travel faster.

Transport routes

With the advent of wheeled vehicles, roads and tracks were built to make journeys easier. These smoothed over any rough surfaces, allowing vehicles to travel faster.

The earliest roads were little more than paths, but these were improved by laying down stones or logs. Roads were widened over the years to carry more and more vehicles. Today's enormous, multi-laned motorways are capable of carrying cars at high speed.

▼ The Romans were great road builders. At the height of their empire, around AD 100, they had about 85 000 km of roads, such as the Appian Way shown here. Some of these are still in use today.

In the 16th century, tracks were used by horse-drawn wagons. The invention of steam trains in the 19th century led to a great increase in track laying. Thousands of kilometres were put down. These linked towns and reduced travelling times from days to hours.

◀ Today, machines do a lot of the work in laying tracks. The first tracks were laid by huge teams of people who did everything, including digging tunnels through whole mountains.

EUREKA!

 In the late 18th and early 19th centuries, John McAdam developed a new way of building roads. He used crushed stones to create a tough, watertight surface. Today, this method is still used, but asphalt or tar is added to bond the stones together.

Era of the train

The development of steam power and, later, diesel and electric motors led to the creation of locomotives to pull trains along railway tracks.

The first steam locomotives were built in the 19th century. These machines could pull long trains carrying people and cargo over vast distances quickly. Railway networks were built to carry materials for growing industries and to connect towns that expanded rapidly in size during this period.

▼ In 1829, the Rocket locomotive, designed by George and Robert Stephenson, won a competition that allowed them to supply trains to run between Manchester and Liverpool in England.

▲ This train is called a monorail because it runs on one track rather than two.

Today, diesel and electric power have all but replaced steam, and trains are longer and faster. There are even vehicles, called maglev trains, that use magnets to hover over the tracks.

LOOK CLOSER

Steam engines use fire to heat water into steam. The steam expands with the heat to create pressure, known as a head of steam. When this pressure is high enough, it can be channelled into a system of pistons that move back and forth to drive the wheels of a locomotive.

Age of the car

Today, the car is a commonplace sight. However, this vehicle is a relatively new invention and was only made possible by the development of a light and powerful engine.

Attempts at fitting steam engines to carts were unsuccessful because the engines were too large to be practical. The development of a suitable engine did not occur until the 1870s, when the gasoline-powered internal-combustion engine was created and used to build the first motorbikes and cars.

▼ One of the first steam-powered carriages was built in 1769 by engineer Nicolas-Joseph Cugnot.

Since the development of the internal-combustion engine, millions of vehicles have been built. The introduction of mass production by companies such as Ford in America, made these vehicles more affordable and available to all.

▲ The increasing use of the car has caused problems such as heavy traffic and air pollution.

LOOK CLOSER

Today, some car manufacturers build cars specifically for our crowded city streets. These cars are small, which makes them easier to park, and they are more fuel-efficient, meaning they are cheaper to run and create less pollution.

Wind and oars

Boats and ships have been used for thousands of years to cross rivers, lakes and oceans. They were one of the first methods of transport to carry passengers and cargo to disant lands.

The earliest boats were used in Ancient Egypt over 6000 years ago. These were powered by oars and simple sails and travelled along the River Nile. Over the years, the numbers of oars and rowers were increased to give the boats more speed.

▼ This is a re-creation of an Ancient Greek ship known as a trireme because it has three rows of oars.

Sailing technology also improved, with new sail shapes and better construction. This allowed people to cross the broadest stretches of ocean. By the middle of the 16th century, sailing ships had circumnavigated the world, making long-distance travel a reality.

▲ Ships with sails are still popular today, but most are equipped with engines to power them if the wind drops.

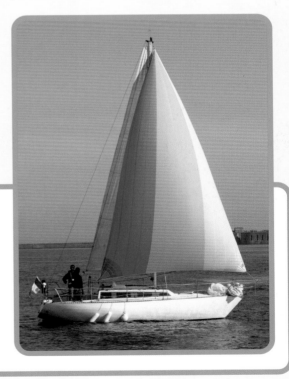

LOOK CLOSER

Modern sailing boats, such as this yacht, use a triangular-shaped sail called a lateen sail. These sails can catch the wind from almost any direction while still pushing a boat forwards. This design was developed by Arab sailors thousands of years ago and copied by European sailors in the Middle Ages.

Powered boats

The development of steam engines provided boats and ships with a reliable source of power. They no longer had to rely on the wind or rowers to propel them forwards.

Towards the end of the 18th century, the first steamboats were being tested in France, Britain and the USA. These early boats travelled up and down rivers and were driven by large paddle wheels turned by a steam engine.

◄ This steamboat from the USA has its paddle wheel at the stern (rear). The paddle wheel spins around to push the boat forward.

EUREKA!

In 1959, British inventor Christopher Cockerell successfully built the world's first hovercraft. It worked by floating on top of a cushion of air trapped by rubber skirts underneath the vehicle. Hovercraft are fast and can travel on both land and sea.

Massive improvements to ships were made during the 19th century. By the end of the century, they were being built of iron instead of wood. Ships were driven by propellers and fitted with powerful diesel engines. Today, some ships, such as oil tankers, are over 450 m long.

▼ The enormous Queen Mary II can carry nearly 4000 passengers and crew. It has a gym, a spa, a planetarium, a casino and a basketball court.

Under the water

Submarines and submersibles can travel both on and below the surface of the water. These vehicles are used to explore the depths of the oceans and for military purposes.

The submarine was first proposed at the end of the 16th century. The earliest working vessel was built by Dutch inventor Cornelius Drebbel in 1620. It travelled under the River Thames in London, England, at depths of 4.5 m. In contrast, modern military submarines can dive to depths of up to 840 m.

◀ The Turtle was built in 1775 and was the first submarine to be used in war. It was designed to attach explosives to the underside of a ship before blowing it up.

The submarine came of age in the two world wars of the 20th century. During these conflicts, submarines attacked enemy ships by firing torpedoes or deck guns. After World War II, submarines used nuclear power, which made them quieter than before and allowed them to stay underwater for longer.

► Modern submarines are fitted with the latest technology which allows them to hide from enemy ships.

Submersibles are small craft used to explore wrecks or study deep-sea plants and animals. Some submersibles do not have a crew and are operated by remote control.

Flying free

Hot-air balloons were the first flying machines. Since then, a variety of aircraft, including gliders, have been developed. These were the forerunners of today's powered aircraft.

The earliest hot-air balloon used air heated by a fire to fill a large fabric bag. The heated air inside the bag was lighter than the air around it, so the balloon rose into the air, lifting a basket suspended underneath.

◄ The first hot-air balloon was built in 1783 by French brothers Joseph-Michel and Jacques-Étienne Montgolfier.

▲ Modern airships, such as this one, are filled with helium gas, which is safer to use than hydrogen.

LOOK CLOSER

Gliders are able to fly because they have wings, like planes. In the air, glider pilots have to look for rising currents of warm air that they can use to raise the glider higher into the air.

Airships – a type of powered balloon – were used as passenger and military craft in the early 20th century. They were filled with hydrogen, a gas that is lighter than air. Hydrogen catches fire easily, and several disasters ended the popularity of the airship.

Powered flight

The age of powered flight began on 17 December 1903, when Orville and Wilbur Wright successfully flew their aeroplane at Kitty Hawk, North Carolina, USA.

Since the Wright brothers' first flight, aircraft have been built in many shapes and sizes for many different uses. World War I (1914–1918) increased the rate of aircraft development, as hundreds were built as fighter or bomber planes.

▼ The first flight by Orville Wright lasted just **12** seconds and covered only **35** m.

▲ The Airbus A380 can carry up to 555 people for nearly 15 000 km without refuelling.

Following World War I, non-military air travel increased when the first passenger airlines were formed and flights began delivering mail. Another great leap forward came with the invention of the jet engine. The jet could power planes farther and faster. Concorde, for example, could fly at 2179 km/h – that's more than twice the speed of sound.

EUREKA!

In 1930, engineer Frank Whittle obtained a patent for a jet engine. Since then, this revolutionary engine has been fitted to military and civilian aircraft to transport people around the world in a matter of hours.

Hovering around

Helicopters have the ability to hover in the air, take off and land vertically, and fly in any direction. This means that they can deliver people and cargo without the need for a long runway.

Unlike a plane, which uses its fixed wings to lift itself off the ground, a helicopter uses a rapidly spinning rotor. The first helicopters were built in the 1930s and people soon recognised how useful these aircraft could be.

◄ Because they can hover and land in tight and difficult spaces without a runway, helicopters are ideal for rescue situations.

◄ This military Chinook helicopter can lift a load of up to 11 tonnes.

After World War II, helicopters were adopted by the armed services and used in conflicts such as those in Vietnam in the 1960s and 70s and in the more recent Gulf Wars. They are also used for civilian purposes such as fighting fires, transporting cargo and carrying passengers.

EUREKA!

The helicopter is not a new idea. Chinese papers dating from AD 400 describe a kite that used a rotating wing to take off. This early sketch of a helicopter design was made in the 15th century by Leonardo da Vinci. The first helicopters were not built for another 500 years.

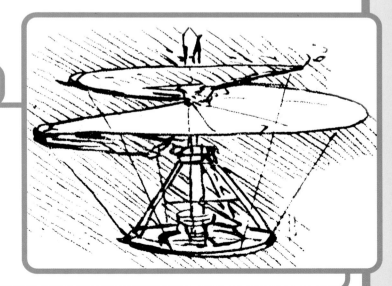

Into space

For hundreds of years, people have dreamt about being transported beyond Earth and into space. Unmanned spacecraft, known as probes, were the first to explore the universe, but people weren't far behind.

The space age started on 4 October 1957 with the launch of *Sputnik 1*. The first person into space was Russian Yuri Gagarin in 1961. America sent its first person into space, Alan Shepard, nearly a month later.

▲ *Sputnik 1* was a metal ball that sent out a simple radio signal as it travelled around the Earth.

▼ The space shuttle is a reusable US space vehicle that carries astronauts and equipment into space.

In July 1969, the first people set foot on the Moon. Since then, many probes have been sent throughout the solar system. Satellites continue to explore space to help us understand more about the universe.

EUREKA!

 Many spacecraft are powered by a rocket engine that uses fuel and oxygen in liquid form. The world's first liquid-fuelled rocket was built by American inventor Robert Goddard. On 16 March 1926, he launched this liquid-fuelled rocket at his aunt's farm in Auburn, Massachusetts, USA.

Timeline

- c. **10 000** BC. Dogs are tamed for the first time and used for carrying possessions and dragging vehicles.

- c. **4000** BC. The earliest evidence of boats show sailing vessels on the River Nile in Ancient Egypt.

- c. **3500** BC. The earliest images of wheels are drawn in Ancient Sumeria, a region that is now in Iraq.

- c. **2000** BC. The first spoked wheels are built.

- **1783.** Joseph-Michel and Jaques-Étienne Montgolfier build the world's first hot-air balloon.

10 000 BC

- c. AD **400.** Chinese documents make the first mention of a helicopter.

- **1796.** Nicolas-Joseph Cugnot builds his steam-powered carriage.

- **1775.** The *Turtle* is the first submarine to be used in warfare in an attack on British warships.

- c. AD **100.** At its height, the Ancient Roman Empire has about 85 000 km of roads.

- **1620.** Cornelius Drebbel builds and sails the world's first submarine.

- 1823. The British government adopts John McAdam's ideas for improving road surfaces.

- 1829. The *Rocket* wins a competition allowing George and Robert Stephenson to supply locomotives for the line between Manchester and Liverpool, England.

- C. 1870. Internal-combustion engines are fitted to the first motorbikes and cars.

- C. 1930 The first helicopters are built.

- 1930. Frank Whittle patents his invention for the jet engine.

- 1937. The airship *Hindenburg* explodes, killing 36 people and ending the popularity of airship travel.

- 2003. Space Shuttle *Columbia* breaks up entering Earth's atmosphere.

- 2004. Mike Melvill becomes the first person to fly a privately built rocket into space.

TODAY

- 1926. Robert Goddard launches the world's first liquid-fuelled rocket.

- 1969. Neil Armstrong is the first person to set foot on the Moon.

- 1959. Christopher Cockerell builds the world's first hovercraft.

- 1957. *Sputnik 1* becomes the first space probe.

- 1903. The Wright brothers make the first powered flight at Kitty Hawk, North Carolina, USA.

Factfile

• The first major road was called the Persian Royal Road. It stretched from the Persian Gulf to the Aegean Sea, a distance of about 2857 km. It was used from 3500 to 300 BC.

• The largest steam locomotive ever built was the Union Pacific *Big Boy*, used in the United States in the 1940s and 1950s. It was more than 40 m long and had wheels that were bigger than an adult.

• The earliest tracks, from around 2000 BC, were just grooves in pathways that helped keep wagons on the road.

• The car built by Carl Benz in 1885 travelled about 1 km at a speed of 15 km/h when it was first demonstrated to the public. In contrast, the land-speed record today is held by *Thrust* SSC, which reached 1227.985 km/h!

• The record for the fastest speed ever achieved on a railway system was set by a French TGV *Atlantique*. It reached a speed of 515.3 km/h.

• *Voyager* 2 holds the record for the most planets visited by a spacecraft. Between 1979 and 1984, it visited Jupiter, Saturn, Uranus and Neptune.

Glossary

Asphalt
A thick, black material that is added to gravel to cover the surface of a road.

Internal-combustion engine
An engine that mixes fuel with air inside a cylinder and ignites this mixture. The resulting explosion causes a piston to move up and down and this movement is transmitted to the wheels of a car.

Locomotive
A self-propelled vehicle that is used to pull trains. Locomotives can be powered by steam, electricity or diesel engines.

Pack animal
An animal that is used to carry or pull goods or people.

Patent
The official document that states the inventor is the only person who can make, use and sell a device.

Piston
A disc or rod that moves up and down inside a cylinder. This movement can be caused by expanding gases in an internal-combustion engine or by steam in a steam engine.

Pollution
Harmful chemical substances that are added to the environment by human actions, such as burning petrol in a car engine.

Propeller
A spinning wheel that is fitted with a number of blades. A propeller is fitted to a boat or an aircraft to push them forwards.

Rocket
An engine in which a mixture of fuel and oxygen is set alight to create a powerful jet of hot gas. This powerful jet pushes a vehicle forwards.

Rotor
On a helicopter, this is a set of blades that spins to produce the lifting force that carries the vehicle into the air.

Sail
A large area of material that is used on a sailing boat to catch the wind and push the vessel forwards.

Spokes
Bars that connect the centre, or hub, of a wheel to the outer rim.

Index